Narratives and the Making of History

Narratives and the Making of History

Two Lectures

Romila Thapar

OXFORD
UNIVERSITY PRESS

OXFORD
UNIVERSITY PRESS

YMCA Library Building, Jai Singh Road, New Delhi 110001

Oxford University Press is a department of the University of Oxford. It furthers the University's objective of excellence in research, scholarship, and education by publishing worldwide in

Oxford New York

Athens Auckland Bangkok Bogota Buenos Aires Calcutta
Cape Town Chennai Dar es Salaam Delhi Florence Hong Kong Istanbul
Karachi Kuala Lumpur Madrid Melbourne Mexico City Mumbai
Nairobi Paris Sao Paolo Singapore Taipei Tokyo Toronto Warsaw

with associated companies in Berlin Ibadan

Published in India
By Oxford University Press, New Delhi

First published 2000

ISBN 019 565 177 4

Typeset in Adobe Garamond
by Jojy Philip, Shalimar Bagh, New Delhi 110 052
Printed by Pauls Press, New Delhi 110020
Published by Manzar Khan, Oxford University Press
YMCA Library Building, Jai Singh Road, New Delhi 110 001

Preface

I would like to thank the Vice-Chancellor of the University of Bombay, Dr Snehalata Deshmukh, as also the Department of History and Dr Mariam Dossal for inviting me to give the D.D. Kosambi Memorial Lectures this year. I deem it a privilege to be associated with a memorial to D.D. Kosambi, whose work was a paradigm shift in early Indian history and has been foundational to the more significant historical analyses of the last few decades. His insights, based both on a meticulous study of texts and an undaunting familiarity with the survival of cultures in the Indian world, have been inspirational to a large range of studies. My lectures today and tomorrow, will be drawing on some of these insights, particularly those from his collection of essays entitled, *Myth and Reality*.

The intention in these two lectures, is to explore one among the many aspects of historical writing, namely, the relationship between narrative and history. Analysing variant versions of other texts have suggested to me the multi-layered links between the creation of a narrative and its context: where the context is in turn multiple involving both the historical moment and perspectives of a longer duration.

I would like to acknowledge helpful discussions of some aspects of these lectures with Professor Muzaffar Alam and Professor Neeladri Bhattacharya. Needless to say the views reflected here, except when otherwise stated, have resulted from my questioning of the sources. I would also like to thank Professor Sushil

Srivastava who drew my attention to the publication of the debate in the House of Commons and very kindly sent me a photocopy of the same. I would particularly like to thank David Nelson, the South Asian Bibliographer in the Van Pelt Library of the University of Pennsylvania, for his unfailing help in making available the varied publications which I have had occasion to consult.

New Delhi
1999

ROMILA THAPAR

Contents

Lecture One
Śakuntalā: Histories of a Narrative 1

Lecture Two
Somanātha: Narratives of a History 24

Index 51

Lecture One

Śakuntalā: Histories of a Narrative

The manner in which we construct the past is now acknowledged as an important process in the writing of history. This involves appropriating the past, an act in which the concerns of the present are apparent. Historical sources are used to construct a link between an event in the past and how we view it today. I would like to argue that there are in addition many representations of an event between the point at which it happened and the present, and that these representations are significant to the eventual understanding of the past. Such representations in the form of a narrative may either be fictional or may claim to embody an event, but in both cases they address themselves to a historical moment. This brings the relationship between narrative and history to the forefront.

In the first lecture I will be looking at this relationship through the different versions of a fictionalized narrative, illustrating my argument with the story of Śakuntalā in its variant forms. Does the retelling of the same narrative help our understanding of historical change in as much as the retelling reflects change in both society and ideology? Can we treat the act of narrativization or the making of a narrative, as constituting an event? Every narrative has a context which is consciously or subconsciously derived from a world view and an ideology. Let me hastily add however, that this is not to authenticate a story as history, for a story remains fictional. But it can reveal perspectives of a time and a society. I am suggesting that it be analysed as representing such a perspective, which emerges all the more clearly through a comparison of its retellings. A fictionalized narrative cannot be treated as history but it can be an indicator of a past condition. What I am arguing for is the analysis of narratives which become constituents of a historical perception and have therefore a contextual location.

A narrative can have its own biography and the changes it manifests can provide us with a view of historical change. By historical change I do not mean just chronology but rather, the manifold dimensions of the historical context. A narrative frequently recreated over time becomes multi-layered like a palimpsest. One can attempt to reveal the many pasts which went into the making of its present. Where the retellings of a narrative or where narratives implying an event, become contesting versions, the differing perspectives also provide evidence for historical constructions. In my second lecture I shall be discussing the many representations of a well-known event — the raid of Mahmud of Ghazni on the temple of Somanātha in 1026 — to see how the event is viewed from various perspectives. The second lecture is therefore in some ways an inversion of the first. The subject matter of the two lectures is not linked, but there is a methodological link in seeing the relationship of narrative to history.

This relationship has been the subject of lively discussion among historians. Best known perhaps was the discussion between Lawrence Stone on the revival of narrative in history and its critique by Eric Hobsbawm, published in the 1980s in the British historical journal, *Past and Present.* The discussions focused largely on whether there was a shift away from social and economic history, drawing on the disciplines of the social sciences, towards directing attention to language, culture and ideas and a focus on micro-events. Was this a new way of viewing the structures of the story and of society? The suggested duality was found to be untenable since there was a considerable over-lap in both sources and interpretations. Even narrative history as it has developed in recent times, was not just a bald telling of a story. The new use of narrative incorporated analytical history and the analyses of the micro-event illumined the macro generalization.

The discussion has taken a different form in this decade with the introduction of what has been termed 'the linguistic turn'.[1] Some have stated that history as a discipline has no future given the kind of analyses of narrative which are possible. History in this argument becomes a kind of *pointillist* history — rather like the style of painting — a collection of unconnected dots which taken together compose a picture. Historians have reacted with the logical argument that even these dots have to be contextualized as indeed does the picture itself. However significant the understanding of the fragments may be, history attempts to look at the larger whole. What 'the linguistic turn' has done is to make historians more aware of the nuances of language and words, which far from terminating historical investigation, have added to its precision.

The writing of history has had a continuous interface with literature. Historians have culled literature for information on what may have happened in the past, the statements being juxtaposed with other kinds of evidence. This is a legitimate activity. I would however suggest a sharpening of this interface by changing the

[1] R.J. Evans, *In Defence of History*, London, 1997.

focus somewhat, by searching for the historical perspectives which this interface provides, through examining the representations present in the narrative. The same narrative or approximately the same, can occur in variant forms as different genres of literature — in this case, the story of Śakuntalā in the *Mahābhārata*, the play of Kālidāsa, the prose-poem in Braja-*bhāṣā*. From a different perspective but with a bearing on the narrative, are the many translations of the Kālidāsa play where the act of translation in itself becomes a cultural negotiation, and there is also the commentary in the form of an essay by Rabindranath Tagore. These are significant moments in the biography of a narrative.

But there is more that just an interface between literature and history. The narrative of Śakuntalā, highlights the gender perspective. The same character is depicted differently in the variant forms. Does this reflect different social perceptions, the understanding of which requires some familiarity with the historical context? The form which the variants take — epic fragment, drama, poetry — and the cultural interpretations which they encourage, makes the narrative an item in cultural history.

Choosing a particular item from the past and recreating it as a variant is in part, an act of historical significance. The past is viewed from the present, wherever the present may be located, and that which is selected from the past goes into constructing a tradition or constructing a history. A tradition is never handed down intact from generation to generation, however appealing this idea may seem. Innovation is what gives it vitality. The items selected from the past are often so chosen as to legitimize the values and codes of the present. In selecting and recasting cultural items we highlight some and marginalize others. The act of selection becomes a dialogue with the past.

The point in time at which the selection is being made gives a different value to the selection as a cultural symbol, as an idiom, as an icon. This has happened throughout our cultural history, although our awareness of this process is perhaps more apparent now. Where the narrative is culturally central to our own present today, we have also to see it as a part of the intervention of the colonial period and recognize the disjuncture this may produce.

The concept of culture in relation to the early past, implies an intersecting of disciplines of which history, it seems to me is foundational. This involves the original text and its historical contexts, as also frequently the Orientalist reading of it and equally frequently, the internalizing of this reading by commentators of the last century or two. And more recently, the questioning of this reading. Inevitably there is a contextualizing of the Orientalist representation and European perspectives brought to bear on the reading. A single item can therefore have multiple identities which change at historical moments. Understanding a cultural item historically requires some comprehension of the world-view which it represented. Each version has some relation with those which preceded it: a relation ranging from endorsement to contestation of earlier versions.

I would like to touch on some of these ideas using the narrative of Śakuntalā. My focus therefore is not on the Kālidāsa play, but on the treatment of the central figure which transforms the narrative in its variant versions; and on the possible historical explanations for the variants and the commentaries.

Let me now turn to the narrative.

The *ākhyāna* or narrative of Śakuntalā as given in the Ādi *parvan* of the *Mahābhārata*[2] is one among the many bardic fragments which were stitched together in the making of the epic. In many

[2] Ādi *parvan* 62–9.

of these fragments the morphology of the folk tale is evident. There are other sections of the *Mahābhārata*, such as the Śānti *parvan*, which have been labelled as didactic. These have less to do with the story and more with theories of the ideal society, of social obligations — *dharma*, of government — *rāja-dharma*, of ideas about the liberation of the soul — *mokṣa-dharma*, and such like. The Śakuntalā story occurs in the narrative section.[3]

Rājā Duḥṣanta, with the title of *goptā*, a protector of cows, has conquered widely. One day he goes on a hunt accompanied by a large entourage of soldiers. The hunt turns into a fierce killing of tigers and deer, the wounding of elephants, the uprooting of trees and a general devastation of nature. Duḥṣanta follows a deer deep into the forest which brings him to the lush and secluded *āśrama* of Kaṇva. On calling out, a young woman answers and performs the ritual of welcome for the guest. She introduces herself as Śakuntalā, the daughter of the *ṛṣi* Kaṇva. On Duḥṣanta asking her how a *ṛṣi* could have daughter, she explains her parentage in detail. Indra, disturbed by the powers which the *ṛṣi* Viśvāmitra was accumulating through *tapasya*, sent the *apsarā* Menakā to seduce him. Śakuntalā was born but discarded by Menakā and brought up as a foundling by Kaṇva in his *āśrama*.

Duḥṣanta, deeply attracted by what he calls 'the flawless girl of the beautiful hips', proposes a *gāndharva* marriage. This was a marriage by mutual consent, appropriate it is said, to *kṣatriyas*. Śakuntalā agrees but sets a condition that she will only marry him if the son born of this marriage is declared his successor. After a three year pregnancy she gives birth to a boy, Bharata. She takes him at a young age to Hastināpura from where Duḥṣanta rules, and demands that Duḥṣanta recognize him as his heir. Duḥṣanta pretends not to recognize her and rejects them both. Śakuntalā in

[3] V.S. Sukthankar, On the meaning of the *Mahābhārata*, Bombay, 1964.

extreme anger, explains why a wife and son are necessary to him, particularly a son to continue the lineage. The exchange is heated with much down-to-earth abuse. Menakā is called a slut. Viśvāmitra a lecher and Śakuntalā a whore. Śakuntalā stands her ground and insists that the boy be given his status and to that end she decides to leave him with Duḥṣanta. As she is about to return to the *āśrama*, a disembodied celestial voice proclaims that the boy is indeed Duḥṣanta's son. Duḥṣanta explains that he had remembered his meeting with her and had no doubt about the veracity of Śakuntalā's claim, but was waiting for this public legitimation of the relationship. Subsequently he accepts them both. Bharata when he comes to rule is acclaimed as a great ruler.

The story in the epic is the origin myth of Bharata and therefore also tied into the ancestry of the Kauravas and the Pāṇḍavas, central to the events in the *Mahābhārata*. Divine proclamation establishes status and legitimacy because the relationship has also to be accepted by the clansmen. It is a society of clans and heroes, a lineage-based society, where ancestry, genealogy and origins are vital.[4] It is also a cattle-keeping society requiring extensive grazing grounds. Hence the respect for the title of *goptā*. The clearing of land and of forest for agriculture was recognized as a source of wealth. The hunt is a surrogate raid, a war against nature but also a means of establishing claims to territory. So dominance over the forest is beginning to assume importance.

The depiction of Śakuntalā is central to the story. She is forthright, free, high-spirited and assertive. She makes her marriage conditional and then demands that the promise be honoured. She accuses Duḥṣanta of behaving unrighteously. She is the reverse of the *pativratā*, the ideal wife as described in the didactic sections of the epic. The dispute is clearly over the paternity of the child. The

[4] Romila Thapar, *From Lineage to State*, Delhi, 1984.

condition she imposed at the time of the *gāndharva* marriage hinged on the status of her son, characteristic of a patriarchal society. This was also crucial to the status of the woman in a such a society even if it was a clan-based society: she was the link to kinship and alliances, and her son ensured her membership of the clan. The celestial voice describes the mother as the receptacle, for it is the father who begets the son, and the son frees the father from the abode of the dead. Implicit in this utterance is the statement that Duḥṣanta accept responsibility for the child.

The period of the composition of the epic remains controversial but generally it is thought that the composition and the interpolations can be placed between 400 BC and AD 400, the narrative sections possibly being earlier than the didactic sections.[5] The epic continues to have an audience well into the centuries AD. It is part of ancestral mythology and provides links with the heroes of old. The epic was added to often enough, and presumably when it was converted to sacred literature it became part of brahmanical high culture. However, the hierarchy in this high culture would have placed the epics and *Purāṇas* in what some regarded as the not-so-high culture, perhaps because of their links with folk culture.

I would now like to turn to the play, the *Abhijñāna-śākuntalam* of Kālidāsa.[6] It reflects a different historical scene. It was written subsequent to the story in the epic and is generally dated to about the fourth century AD although the date is controversial. Kālidāsa selects a fragment from the epic, converts the narrative into a

[5] Sukthankar, op. cit.

[6] M.R. Kale, The *Abhijñāna-śākuntalam* of Kālidāsa, Bombay, 1961. A discussion and translation of the play is included in B. Stoler Miller (ed.), *Theater of Memory*, New York, 1984.

nāṭaka/a play, which is a different genre of literature from the poetry of the epic. To the original narrative he adds other sub-themes. One is the story of the ring as a token of recognition which seems to have come from the Buddhist *Kaṭṭahāri Jātaka*.[7] The other is the theme of the curse which is frequent in folk literature. There is, as a result, the creating of a new tradition. An item, selected from the past, is moulded to suit the cultural expression of the later time. It could be seen almost as a contestation with the epic version, the norms of which undergo changes in the play.

The play is no longer concerned with lineage-based societies and clans but carries the rhetoric of the political power of monarchical states. These were well established, legitimizing the concentration of power in a single family and the authority of upper caste society. The state had its appurtenances of administration, revenue, coercive agencies and such like. There is also the visibility of brahmanical high culture which was dominant in the construction of classicism and therefore familiar to Kālidāsa. It is evident in the use of language and in the nuanced relationship between the characters. Kingship is approximate to deity and kings and gods intermingle. The *āśrama* of the Kaṇvas carries traces of a new incipient institution which was to develop into the *agrahāras* of post-Gupta times, institutions which changed the socio-economic landscape. Tax-free land was donated by the king for settlement by *brāhmaṇas* which could be in areas already under cultivation or newly opened to cultivation. These were to become powerful nuclei and networks of brahmanical culture.

The play itself is intended for performance at the court before a small, sophisticated, urban audience and not as part of a popular

[7] E.B. Cowell (ed.), *The Jātakas*, vol. I, no. 7, London, 1969 (repr.) See also Stoler Miller, op. cit.

recitation. It reflects the values of upper caste society although there may implicitly on occasion be some questioning of these. Intended as entertainment, the theme was inevitably romantic.

The changes introduced by Kālidāsa are significant to more than just the story-line. Duḥṣanta/Duṣyanta leaves his ring with Śakuntalā as a token of his promise to send for her on his return to Hastināpura. Deep in thought one day, Śakuntalā neglects to receive with appropriate ceremony an irascible *ṛṣi* Durvāsas who therefore spews out his curse that the person she is thinking of will not remember her. Her friends plead for at least a modification of the curse and the *ṛṣi* then says that the ring will provide the remembrance. Śakuntalā leaves for the court and on the way loses the ring. On arriving there, she is not recognized by Duḥṣanta and no amount of persuasion convinces him that she is his legally wedded wife bearing his son. Śakuntalā in despair calls upon Mother Earth and there is a flash of lightening and she is whisked away to the *āśrama* of Mārīca. Here she gives birth to her son Bharata. Meanwhile the ring is found in the belly of a fish, and since it is his signet ring, it is brought to Duḥṣanta. On seeing it he recollects his relationship with Śakuntalā. He is now full of remorse at having lost both a wife and a son. The eventual happy outcome occurs when the king is called to Indra's aid in a campaign against the demons. On his return he stops at the *āśrama* of Mārīca where he is united with his wife and son.

The story of the play is an elaboration of the skeletal story in the epic. Courtly drama requires a romantic mood and dramatic effects. The teasing out of the narrative is done through the sub-plots of the curse and the ring. There is a contrapuntal relationship between the two; the curse impedes action and is a barrier, the ring resolves the barrier so that the action can move.

The curse and the ring gloss over the tension between Duḥṣanta and Śakuntalā, both over the paternity of the child and the responsibility of the father. But Śakuntalā in the play cannot defend the right of her son because the flow of events is beyond human control and she had made no conditions to the marriage. Duḥṣanta cannot be blamed for rejecting her as he is under a spell. Is Kālidāsa therefore avoiding the moral issue of condemning Duḥṣanta's action in rejecting Śakuntalā? Or would this not have been regarded as irresponsible in those times and in that society? The epic version does at least raise the issue through the celestial voice.

The structure of the play seems to be based on a duality which comes to be associated with an increasingly common view of the world. It is expressed in terms of the dichotomy of the *grāma* and the *araṇya* or the *kṣetra* and the *vana* — the settlement and the forest.[8] It is generic to the epic where the broader action moves back and forth from settlement to forest. But it is strongly indented in the play as well. One of the reasons for this may be that by the Gupta period attitudes towards the forest were beginning to change. Whereas earlier the settlement was the ordered society and the forest the habitat of the unknown, and the wild, now the forest was beginning to be seen differently: as a source of revenue through its natural products of timber and elephants; its potential as agricultural land after clearing; and as the location of *brāhmaṇa* settlements, in the form of *agrahāras*. The society of the forest was no longer entirely unknown, but it was still different from village settlements and the difference continued to be emphasized.

The dichotomy is highlighted in the play between the *āśrama* of Kaṇva and the court at Hastināpura. It is further underlined in the depiction of Śakuntalā as the woman of the *āśrama* and

[8] C. Malamoud, *Cooking the World*, Delhi, 1996, 87–8; 'Village et Fôret dans l'Ideologie de l'Inde Brahmanique', *Archives Sociologie Européene*, July 1976.

Duhṣanta as the man of the court. The *āśrama* in the play is the liminal area, the threshold between the settlement and the forest, for although it is set deep in the forest, the people who live there attuned to nature, are nevertheless also aware of the mores and customs of the settled society, from where they have come. They are not *āṭavikas*, forest dwellers, in origin.

Kālidāsa seems to use this duality to reverse the activities associated with each. The *āśrama* becomes the location for what has been called love-in-union — *saṃbhoga śṛṅgāra*, generally not associated with *āśramas*. The court is the location for love-in-separation — *vipralamba śṛṅgāra*, where she is rejected and leaves, although most romances achieve fruition at the court.[9]

From the epic narrative to the play there is a change in the conceptualizing of the woman. Śakuntalā is now the child of nature and identifies with plants and animals. She dresses in bark clothes, adorns herself with flowers which miraculously turn into jewels at the time of her departure. Nature weeps at her going away. Her innocence is heightened by her grappling with the emotions of romantic love, leading her to the *gāndharva* marriage. She is shy, retiring, modest and generally submissive. In the last act she excuses Duhṣanta's action because of his being under a spell, and instead explains to herself that she is reaping the consequences of some wrong doing on her part in a previous birth.

If Śakuntalā claims to be the wife of Duhṣanta she has to conform to the *pativratā* ideal. Although both Kaṇva and Duhṣanta refer to her as the lawfully wedded wife, one of Kaṇva's disciples hints at the *gāndharva* marriage being a seduction. One wonders whether this is resentment against a woman's transgression of patriarchy and her taking an independent decision, for he insists that she must suffer the consequences of such a decision.

[9] B. Stoler Miller, op. cit.

She is told that she cannot return to the *āśrama* and has to remain at the court because the husband's authority over the wife is unlimited. He has the right to accept her or abandon her. It is better that a wife be a servant in her husband's home than live away from him.

The epic version had underlined the centrality of the son and the empowerment of the woman, both in herself and as the mother of a son. In the play romantic love seems to supersede this, and the question of empowerment fades away. The king does not taunt her for her illegitimacy but is uncomplimentary about women in general. Eventually the desire for an heir drives the king to as much grief as the disappearance of his beloved.

Subsequent to the Kālidāsa play there were now two versions of the story in circulation. Briefly narrated in the *Purāṇas* as an ancestral myth of the Pūrus it was important to the legitimation of dynasties of the post-Gupta period.[10] The recitations of the *paurānikas* and the *kathākāras* kept these stories alive among audiences more comfortable with the oral tradition. That it became something of a folk stereotype is evident from the *Kathāsarītasagāra* which includes a charming story using the same theme but replete with folk motifs.[11] Interpretations of visual forms as pictorial representations of the story have also been suggested.[12]

[10] E.g. *Bhāgavata Purāṇa*, 9.20.7–32; *Matsya Purāṇa*, 49, 11–15.

[11] C.H. Tawney, (ed. and tr.), 1968 (repr.), *The Kathāsarītasāgara*, Ch. XXXII, 306–90.

[12] V.S. Agrawala, 'Vāsavadattā and Śakuntalā: Scenes in the Ranigumpha cave in Orissa', *Journal of the Indian Society of Oriental Art*, 14, 1946, 102–9; C. Rapin, *Indian Art from Afghanistan*, Delhi, 1996; J.H. Marshall, 'Excavations at Bhita', *ASIAR*, 1911–12, Calcutta, 1915, 29–49, Plates XXIII–XXIV, No. 17.

At a somewhat later period the play becomes an item for discussion in a variety of theoretical works on literature and aesthetics. Taking off from the *Nātyaśāstra*, there were wide-ranging views on what constitutes good poetry and drama, discussed in the works of theoreticians such as Abhinavagupta and Ānanadavardhana at the end of the first millennium AD. More specific to the Kālidāsa play is the commentary of Rāghavabhaṭṭa in the sixteenth century. Much of the discussion was in the context of the evolving theories of *rasa*, central to Indian aesthetics. Gradually the Kālidāsa play became central to analysing both poetry and drama and was judged as the exemplar in the Sanskrit *nāṭaka* tradition.

It was doubtless both its reputation as the finest Sanskrit play and the popularity of the story, that led to its being adapted to yet another literary form which was to reach a still wider audience. In 1716, the Mughal emperor Farrukh Siyar bestowed a title on a nobleman at the court. To celebrate this, the court poet, Navāz Kavīśvara, was asked to render — not to translate — the story of Śakuntalā from Sanskrit into Braj-*bhāṣā*, the language of much of the Hindi poetry at the time. The story now becomes a *kathā* in verse. The theme of love and separation and the style of the rendering, gives it a quality which recalls the dominant form in Braj poetry at that time — the *bārahmāsā*. This is not to suggest that it was actually a *bārahmāsā*, but shorn of the borrowings from the play, it was a *kathā* concerned with lovers, partings and reunions, characteristic of this kind of Braj poetry.[13] The language is earthy, the poetry sounds like doggerel verse at times. Śakuntalā emerges as less given to romanticism and more down-to-earth, a

[13] C. Vaudville, *Bārahmāsā in Indian Literature*, Delhi, 1986; 'A Note on the *Ghataparkara* and the *Meghaduta*', JOI(B), 1959, 9, 2, 129–34.

distinct echo of the Śakuntalā of the epic. In some ways this is a mediation between the epic version and the play.

In 1806, the Braj-*kathā* was translated into an Urdu prose-poem, *Shakuntala*, by Mirza Qasim Ali Dehlavi, an Urdu poet teaching at the recently established Fort William College at Calcutta. This brings an infusion of the Persian *dāstān* style with its world of fables and exaggerated emotions. Śakuntalā, in embarrassment, constantly hides behind her *ghunghat*, and the king in true Majnu or Farhad style, swoons almost every time he sees her. But the dialogue remains earthy and the exchanges between the king and Śakuntalā make for racy reading. The narrative moves away from being a court play and its more accessible language gives it a greater universality. Presumably its performance was accompanied by music, dance and mime. The feel of eighteenth century late Mughal society pervades this version.

At this point, the biography of this narrative takes another turn. There are no further literary genres for the retellings, but it entered the world stage through translations. And translation changes the cultural role of the narrative, for it introduces into the play, the culture and the world views of the society using the language of the translation and of its ideologies.

William Jones, often described as the father of British Indology, was an officer of the East India Company at Calcutta, and spent much time in reading and translating Sanskrit texts. He was enthused by the play, and translated it, first into Latin which was linguistically closer to Sanskrit, and then from Latin into English. In 1789 it was published as *Shakoontala or the Fatal Ring.*[14] He

[14] G. Canon and S. Pandey, 'Sir William Jones Revisited: On His Translation of the Śākuntalā', *JAOS*, 1976, 96, 4, 530–37; G. Canon, *The Life and Mind of Oriental Jones*, Cambridge, 1977; S.N. Mukherjee, *Sir William Jones*, Delhi, 1987 (2nd edn).

gave currency to the phrase that Kālidāsa was the Indian Shakespeare. He maintained that the play demonstrates the height of Indian civilization, all the more remarkable because it was written at a time when the Britons were as unpolished and unlettered as the army of Hanuman. His more significant comment was that he had been disturbed by some of the more erotic passages which would be unacceptable to European taste. And for the first time, the erotic in the play became a matter for debate.

Nevertheless, the play took Europe by storm. It was translated into German and acclaimed by the German poet Goethe in a verse which has since been repeated *ad nauseum*. There followed a succession of ballets and operas on the theme, including an incomplete attempt by Frans Schubert. In each decade of the nineteenth century there was yet another translation in yet another language, even Icelandic. The experimental theatre of Tairoff in Moscow made it the opening presentation with an enthusiastic reception from the Symbolist poets, just prior to the Bolshevik revolution.

Throughout the nineteenth century in European literary circles, and most particularly in the German Romantic Movement, Śakuntalā was projected as the child of nature and the ideal Indian woman encapsulating the beauty of woman kind.[15] Her closeness to nature was particularly important to literary Romanticism distancing itself from the formalism of neo-classicism. This was also in part a response to what was referred to as the 'discovery' of the orient or the Oriental Renaissance. European Romanticism was inter-twined with Orientalism. To understand the construction of Orientalism and its fusion with European Romanticism, requires a familiarity with the images, created as part of the intellectual history of Europe in the nineteenth century, and the politics of

[15] A. Leslie Willson, *A Mythical Image: The Ideal of India in German Romanticism*, Durham, 1964; J. Sedlar, *India in the Mind of Germany*, Washington, 1982; H. Drew, *India and the Romantic Imagination*, Delhi, 1987.

these images. The Oriental Renaissance it was believed, would provide new visions of how man should perceive the world.[16] But the images were what Europe projected onto the Orient. These were crystalized as the duality of the Orient and of Europe as expressed in the preference of Romanticism for the less orderly aspect of the past and its search for the exotic, the irrational, and the imaginative as against the rational and the real, thought to be typical of European classicism.

The creation of what has been called the ideal of India in German Romanticism was also conditioned by early Greek stories of Alexander of Macedon's meetings with Indian philosophers. This was said to explain the presence in substratum European thought of ideas on metempsychosis, the unity of man and nature, and the meaning of renunciation. These were central to the theories of the Neo-Platonists who believed that much of the philosophy alternative to the Judaeo-Christian tradition in Europe, came from Indian sources. Romanticism therefore was also questioning the theories of the European mainstream.

With the growth of notions of race and the wide acceptance of what came to be called 'race science' in the later nineteenth century, a touch of racism entered the idyllic picture of a closeness to nature.[17] The children of nature were the primitive peoples, at the foot of the evolutionary ladder. Eroticism therefore was an aspect of their unawareness of the need for moral laws.

But the not-so-idyllic relationship between colonizers and the colonized in the nineteenth century contributed to a fading out of the enthusiasm for Romanticism. If in the early nineteenth century there was a concern to reform the native to the ways of the

[16] R. Schwab, *The Oriental Renaissance: Europe's Rediscovery of India and the East, 1680–1880*, New York, 1984 (trans.).

[17] T.B. Hanson, 'Inside the Romanticist Episteme', *Thesis Eleven*, 1997, 48, 21–41.

colonizer, by the latter part of the century this was seen as an impossibility because the native was believed to be racially inferior. By the end of the nineteenth century, Śakuntalā had become a collector's item in Europe.

Not so in India. It was in the nineteenth century that the play became important both to debates on colonial cultural policy and to the self-definition of the Indian middle-class. James Mill, writing as a liberal utilitarian, in the early nineteenth century, saw little that was worthwhile in Indian culture, opposed Orientalism, and argued that Sanskrit literature was the literature of a self-indulgent society. It is only nations in their infancy who produce literature which is in praise of the pastoral, for such societies are fettered by despots and they can only indulge in light romances, rather than analysing their condition. The *gāndharva* marriage, the curse, the authority of the *brāhmaṇas*, were for him, signs of Indian degradation.[18]

But there was a tradition among British administrators with a bent for scholarship and working in India, of a more ambiguous view. They felt that those who governed India had to be familiar with its culture and this coincided with forms of exercising power. The so-called 'rediscovery' of the Indian past was in part directed towards this end. But it was also an attempt to revive Indian culture in the format of Orientalist scholarship. This is perhaps best stated in the introduction to yet another translation of the play, published by Monier-Williams in 1855, which superseded the translation of Jones. Where Jones in his writing was representing India both to the Indians and to Europe, now there was a subordination of cultural representation to the politics of

[18] J. Mill, 1823, *History of British India*, London, II. 2. 111.

governance. The attempt was to mould the Indian understanding of its cultural past in the way in which the colonizer intended.[19]

Monier-Williams states in the Introduction to the eighth edition of his translation published in 1898, that it was intended for a variety of purposes. It would enable the British to familiarize themselves with the life of the Hindus. It was also part of British policy to rediscover the Indian past for the Indian, to revive Indian culture as defined by Orientalist scholarship, to make the Indian middle-class aware of this culture and to imprint on the mind of the Indian middle-class, the interpretation given to the culture by Orientalist scholarship. The impression conveyed is that the acclamation for the play should be attributed to Orientalist scholarship, thus forgetting or ignoring, the extensive analyses of earlier literary theorists who wrote some centuries before.

There was now a shift of emphasis and the play was viewed as an item of Hindu culture, explaining the condition of the Hindu subjects of the empire. The reading of the play was moving from Śakuntalā being the child of nature to her being what Monier-Williams calls, the 'rustic maiden'. Nature and culture were no longer juxtaposed for nature had receded and the mores of 'civilization' had become essential to assessing the actions of the play. Initially the play was not selected as a text for the teaching of Sanskrit at college level because it was said to support immorality. Eventually the supposedly erotic passages were deleted and it came to be prescribed. Implicit in this argument is the question of morality — but it is not a comment on the moral decision on which the earlier tradition had focused, that of Duḥṣanta's rejection of Śakuntalā. The question of morality as related to eroticism, which had not been a concern earlier, was now made the central issue and impinged on the projection of Śakuntalā.

[19] G. Visvanathan, 1989, *Masks of Conquest*, New York, 121 ff.

These ideas had an influence on the emerging Indian middle class. Nineteenth century nationalism in India is thought to have fostered a conservative attitude towards tradition, because to question it was a concession to western ideas.[20] The broader middle-class codes were also being forged with the emergence of a new class, associated with the upper castes. These drew from both the new historical situation of colonialism and what was described as the Indian tradition. But in relation to the perspective on women in society, the particular conservatism of Victorian morals had also entered Indian society. There was an appropriation of some of the attitudes of the Judaeo-Christian tradition, attitudes generally absent in early Indian texts. Gradually the definition of womanly virtues focused on modesty, chastity, self-sacrifice, devotion and patience. These were the virtues recognized in the Śakuntalā of the play but these would have been unfamiliar to the Śakuntalā of the epic.

In a later phase of nationalism, a certain liberalism towards women was encouraged and women began to tentatively assert what they saw as their rights. Participation in the national movement was not intended to emancipate women but to encourage a sense of partnership. With rare exceptions, most women remained the subordinate partners. Victorian attitudes and social conservatism could not be set aside so easily.

It was only a matter of time therefore, before someone would declare Śakuntalā's actions as 'the fall of Śakuntalā'. What is surprising is that this comment comes from Rabindranath Tagore. In 1907 he published an essay in Bengali which was later translated

[20] P. Chatterjee, 'The Nationalist Resolution of the Women's Question', in Kumkum Sangari and Sudesh Vaid (eds), *Recasting Women*, Delhi, 1993; 'Colonialism, Nationalism and Coloured Women: The Contest in India', *American Ethnologist*, 1989, 16, 4, 622–33; K. Jayawardena, *The White Woman's Other Burden*, London, 1995.

into English with the title, 'Sakuntala: Its Inner Meaning'.[21] He takes Goethe's verse on Śakuntalā as his starting point and argues that the play is a series of developments from the lesser to the finer, from the flower to the fruit, earth to heaven and matter to spirit. From a young, passionate woman Śakuntalā becomes the model of a devoted wife with qualities of reserve, endurance of sorrow, rigid discipline and piety. According to him, the play focuses on two unions: one is the gross, earthy, physical union with desire contributing to the fall of Śakuntalā — and he uses the words *patana* and *patita* in association with her actions; and the other is the moral union when both Duḥṣanta and Śakuntalā have been cleansed through a long period of separation. Their *tapasya* takes the form of grief, remorse and penance and is necessary to a true and eternal union. Love is not its own highest glory, for goodness is the final goal of love.

This is Tagore's reading of the inner meaning of the play and he sees it as an allegory. Tagore's reading reflects the moral concerns of his time, influenced it would seem by the perspectives of Indian nationalism and also Orientalism. In this reading the empowerment of a woman through the birth of her son, which was significant to the epic story, now becomes unimportant. The woman's morality is the central question.

Let me return to the relationship of narrative and history. If I am reading history into the context of the different versions and commentaries, it is because they are distinct in form and ideology, and when seen in sequence, represent historical changes. I have tried to demonstrate the interface between literature and history not by limiting myself to garnering historical information from

[21] *Modern Review*, 1911, IX, 171 ff.

the texts but by trying to see the texts as representing historical contexts. I have tried to show that the narrative of Śakuntalā changes, either in itself, or through the many translations of one version, and it becomes an icon of varying concerns. Underlying the sequence is what seems to me to be a transformation of these concerns from earlier times to colonial times: a transformation which shifts the focus quite strikingly. Its visibility is clearest in the treatment of gender.

This is evident in the portrayal of Śakuntalā. She is ostensibly the same character in the variant versions but is in effect, perceived differently in each. The perception is not unrelated to a shifting social and moral focus of the story, shifting in accordance with historical demands. She is the mother of an epic hero in the *Mahābhārata* where the main issue is the paternity of her child and the father's responsibility in recognizing this. In the play she is the romantic ideal of upper-caste high culture, where moral responsibility is misted over by the introduction of the extraneous factors of the curse and the ring. In the Braj-*bhāṣā kathā*, she is not cowed down by the king — if anything it may be the reverse — and insists on his behaving in a just manner. German Romanticism sees her as the child of nature, the personification of innocence and pays little attention to problems of paternity and responsibility. The 'rustic maiden' from the colonial perspective, becomes enmeshed in colonial readings of the erotic in the culture of the colonized. The ideal wife within a nationalism reaching back to what it sees as tradition, raises the question of morality but the problem now devolves around the woman always having to exercise restraint. This is a middle-class perspective since subaltern perspectives remain outside the picture.

I have tried to show that each version comes out of a process of selection and implicit in this is the contemporizing of the icon. We select from the past those images which we want from the present. These contribute to the construction of the self-image of our contemporary culture and its projection back into what is believed to be 'tradition'. From the gender perspective we have in the last two centuries, ignored the Śakuntalā of the *Mahābhārata*, the liberated woman demanding to be justly treated, and have endorsed the Śakuntalā of Kālidāsa, the woman waiting patiently for a recognition of her virtue.

Lecture Two

Somanātha: Narratives of a History

In the first lecture, I spoke about a narrative and how its retellings as well as the commentaries on it, can be used to illumine the historical times when these were written; and the historical context in turn can illumine the retelling or the commentary. In this lecture I shall start with a well-known event, and discuss the diverse narratives which contribute to constructing its representations in history. The second theme is in some senses an inversion of the first. It is the use of narrative in history, but in a different way from the first, although the focus is again on retellings or alternative tellings around an event and therefore of a different kind from those which I discussed in the first lecture.

In 1026, Maḥmūd of Ghazni raided the temple of Somanātha and broke the idol. Reference is made to this in various sources, or, reference is omitted where one expects to find it. Some of the references contradict each other. Some lead to our asking questions which do not conform to what we have accepted so far in terms of the meaning and the aftermath of the event. As I mentioned in the first lecture, an event can get encrusted with interpretations from century to century and this changes the perception of the event. As historians therefore, we have to be aware not just of the event and how we look upon it today, but also the ways in which the event was interpreted through the intervening centuries. The analysis of these sources and the priorities in explanation stem of course from the historian's interpretation.

I would like to place before you five representations of this and other events at Somanātha, keeping in mind the historical question of how Maḥmūd's raid was viewed. They cover a wide span and are major representations. The five are the accounts originating from Turko-Persian concerns, Jaina texts of the period, Sanskrit inscriptions from Somanātha, the debate in the British House of Commons and what is often described as a nationalist reading of the event.

Let me begin with a brief background to Somanātha itself. It is referred to in the *Mahābhārata* as Prabhās, and although it had no temple until later, it was a place of pilgrimage, a *tīrtha* — also associated with Kṛṣṇa and the Pāṇḍavas.[1] As was common to many parts of the sub-continent there were a variety of religious sects established in the area — Buddhist, Jaina, Śaiva and Muslim. Some existed in succession and some conjointly. The Śaiva temple, known as the Somanātha temple at Prabhās, dates to about the ninth or tenth century AD.[2] The Caulukyas or Solankis were the ruling dynasty in Gujarat during the eleventh to thirteenth centuries. Kathiawar was administered by lesser *rājās* some of whom were subordinates of the Caulukyas.

Saurashtra was agriculturally fertile, but even more than that, its prosperity came from trade, particularly maritime trade. The

[1] *Vana parvan* 13. 14: 80. 78; 86. 18–19; 119. 1.

[2] B.K. Thapar, 'The Temple at Somanātha: History by Excavations', in K.M. Munshi, *Somnath: The Shrine Eternal*, Bombay, 1951, 105–33; M.A. Dhaky and H.P. Sastri, *The Riddle of the Temple at Somanātha*, Varanasi, 1974.

port at Somanātha, known as Veraval, was one of the three major ports of Gujarat. During this period western India had a conspicuously wealthy trade with ports along the Arabian peninsula and the Persian Gulf.[3] The antecedents of this trade go back many centuries. The Arab conquest of Sind was less indelible than the more permanent contacts based on trade. Arab traders and shippers settled along the west coast, married locally and were ancestors to many communities existing to the present. Some Arabs took employment with local rulers and Rāṣṭrakūta inscriptions speak of Tājika administrators and governors in the coastal areas.[4] The counterparts to these Arab traders were Indian merchants based at Hormuz and at Ghazni, who, even after the eleventh century, are described as extremely prosperous.[5]

The trade focused on the importing of horses from west Asia and also included wine, metal, textiles and spices. The most lucrative was the trade in horses.[6] Funds from temples formed a sizeable investment according to some sources.[7] Port towns such as Somanātha–Veraval and Cambay derived a handsome income from this trade, much of it doubtless being ploughed back to enlarge the profits. Apart from trade, another source of local income were the large sums of money collected in pilgrim taxes by the administration in Somanātha. This was a fairly common source of revenue for the same is mentioned in connection with

[3] V.K. Jain, 1990, *Trade and Traders in Western India*, Delhi.

[4] *Epigraphia Indica*, XXXII, 47 ff.

[5] Muhammad Ulfi, *Jami-ul-Hikayat*, in Eliot and Dowson, *The History of India as Told by Its Own Historians* II, 201. Wasa Ābhīra from Anahilvada had property worth ten lakhs in Ghazni: impressive, even if exaggerated.

[6] Abdullah Wassaf, *Tazjiyat-ul-Amsar*, in Eliot and Dowson, *The History of India as Told by Its Own Historians*, III, 31 ff. Marco Polo also comments on the wealth involved in the horse trade especially with southern India. *Prabandha-cintamani*, 14; Rajasekhara, *Prabandhakosa*, Santiniketan, 1935, 121.

[7] Abdullah Wassaf, Eliot and Dowson, op. cit., I, 69; Pehoa Inscription, *Epigraphia Indica*, 1. 184 ff

the temple at Multan.[8] We are also told that the local *rājās* — the Cūḍasamas, Ābhīras, Yādavas and others — attacked the pilgrims and looted them of their donations intended for the Somanātha temple. In addition there was heavy piracy in the coastal areas indulged in by the local Chāvḍa *rājās* and a variety of sea brigands referred to as the Bawarij.[9] As with many areas generating wealth in earlier times, this part of Gujarat was also subject to unrest and the Caulukya administration spent much time and energy policing attacks on pilgrims and traders.

Despite all this, trade flourished. Gujarat in this period experienced what can perhaps be called a renaissance culture of the Jaina mercantile community. Rich merchant families were in political office, controlled state finance, were patrons of culture, were scholars of the highest order, were liberal donors to the Jaina *saṅgha* and builders of magnificent temples.

This is the backdrop as it were, to the Somanātha temple which by many accounts suffered a raid by Maḥmūd in 1026. There is one sober, contemporary reference and this comes not surprisingly, from Alberuni, a central Asian scholar deeply interested in India, writing extensively on what he observed and learnt. He tells us that there was a stone fortress built about a hundred years before Maḥmūd's raid, within which the *liṅgam* was located — presumably to safe-guard the wealth of the temple. The idol was especially venerated by sailors and traders, not surprising considering the importance of the port at Veraval, trading as far as Zanzibar and China. He comments in a general way on the economic devastation caused by the many raids of Maḥmūd. Alberuni also mentions that Durlabha of Multan, presumably a mathematician, used a round about way involving various eras, to compute the

[8] A. Wink, *Al-Hind*, volume 1, Delhi, 1990, 173 ff; 184 ff; 187 ff.

[9] Alberuni in E.C. Sachau, *Alberuni's India*, New Delhi, 1964 (reprint), I.208.

year of the raid on Somanātha as Śaka 947 (equivalent to AD 1025–6).[10] The raid therefore was known to local sources.

Not unexpectedly, the Turko-Persian chronicles indulge in elaborate myth-making around the event, some of which I shall now relate. A major poet of the eastern Islamic world, Farrukhī Sīstānī, who claims that he accompanied Maḥmūd to Somanātha, provides a fascinating explanation for the breaking of the idol.[11] This explanation has been largely dismissed by modern historians as too fanciful, but it has a significance for the assessment of iconoclasm. According to him the idol at Somanātha was not of a Hindu deity but of a pre-Islamic Arabian goddess. He tells us that the name Somnat (as it was often written in Persian) is actually, Su-manat — the place of Manāt. We know from the *Qur'ān* that Lāt, Uzza and Manāt were the three pre-Islamic goddesses widely worshipped,[12] and the destruction of their shrines and images it was said, had been ordered by the prophet Mohammad. Two were destroyed, but Manāt was believed to have been secreted away to Gujarat and installed in a place of worship. According to some descriptions Manāt was an aniconic block of black stone, so the form could be similar to a *liṅgam*. This story hovers over many of the Turko-Persian accounts, some taking it seriously, others being less emphatic and insisting instead that the icon was of a Hindu deity.

In the thirteenth century, the famous Persian poet Sa'dī provides a garbled description.[13] He claims to have visited the Somanātha temple, although there is no other mention of this.

[10] Ibid., II.9–10, 54.

[11] F. Sīstānī in M. Nazim, 1931, *The Life and Times of Sultan Maḥmūd of Ghazni*, Cambridge.

[12] *Qur'ān*, 53. 19–20. G. Ryckmans, 1951, *Les Religions Arabes Pre-Islamique*, Louvain.

[13] Sa'dī *Bustan* in A.H. Edwards, 1911, *The Bustān of Sadi*, London, 109. Quoted in R.H. Davis, *Lives of Indian Images*, New Jersey, 1997, 100 ff.

According to him the idol was of ivory and decorated like the idol of Manāt — a faultless, female form. It hands moved magically, but when he secretly investigated this, it turned out that they were attached by string to the hands of a person standing behind the idol who worked their movements. According to him the rituals were conducted by priests who came from Iran. This is obviously the fantasy of a poet who has combined the story of Manāt, information on string puppets and rumours of some *brāhmaṇas* having associations with Iran and with the worship of the sun, perhaps confusing Somanātha with the sun-temple at Multan.

The identification of the Somanātha idol with that of Manāt has little historical credibility. There is no evidence to suggest that the temple housed an image of Manāt. Nevertheless the story is significant to the reconstruction of the aftermath of the event, since it is closely tied to the kind of legitimation which was being projected for Maḥmūd.

The link with Manāt added to the acclaim for Maḥmūd. Not only was he the prize iconoclast in breaking Hindu idols, but, in destroying Manāt, he had carried out what were said to be the very orders of the Prophet. He was therefore doubly a champion of Islam.[14] Other temples are raided by him and their idols broken, but Somanātha receives special attention in all the accounts of his activities. Writing of his victories to the Caliphate, Maḥmūd presents them as major accomplishments in the cause of Islam. And not surprisingly Maḥmūd becomes the recipient of grandiose titles. This establishes his legitimacy in the politics of the Islamic world, a dimension which is overlooked by those who see his activities only in the context of northern India.

But his legitimacy also derives from the fact that he was a Sunni and he attacked Ismā'īlīs and Shias whom the Sunnis regarded as

[14] Nazim, op. cit.

heretics.[15] It was ironic that the Ismā'īlīs attacked the temple of Multan and were in turn attacked by Maḥmūd in the eleventh century and their mosque was shut down. The fear of the heretic was due to the popularity of heresies against orthodox Islam and political hostility to the Caliphate in the previous couple of centuries, none of which would be surprising given that Islam in these areas was a relatively new religion. Maḥmūd is said to have desecrated their places of worship at Multan and Manṣūra. His claims to having killed fifty thousand *kāfirs* — infidels, is matched by similar claims to his having killed fifty thousand Muslim heretics. The figure appears to be notional. Maḥmūd's attacks on the Hindus and on the Shias and Ismā'īlīs, was a religious crusade against the infidel and the heretic. But interestingly, these were also the places and peoples involved in the highly profitable horse trade with the Arabs and the Gulf. Both the Muslim heretics of Multan and the Hindu traders of Somanātha had substantial commercial investments. Is it possible then that Maḥmūd, in addition to religious iconoclasm, was also trying to terminate the import of horses into India via Sind and Gujarat? This would have curtailed the Arab monopoly over the trade. Given the fact that there was a competitive horse trade with Afghanistan through north-western India, which was crucial to the wealth of the state of Ghazni, Maḥmūd may well have been combining iconoclasm with trying to obtain a commercial advantage.[16]

In the subsequent and multiple accounts — and there are many in each century — the contradictions and exaggerations increase. There is no agreement on the form of the image. Some say that it is a *liṅgam*, others reverse this and describe it as anthropomorphic — a human form.[17] But even with this there is no consistency as

[15] Wink, op. cit., 184–9; 217–18.
[16] Cf. Mohammad Habib, *Sultan Maḥmūd of Ghazni, Delhi, 1967.*
[17] Ibn Attar quoted in Nazim, op. cit.; Ibn Asir in *Gazetteer of the Bombay*

to whether it is a female Manāt or a male Śiva. There seems to have been almost a lingering wish that it might be Manāt. Was the icon, if identified with Manāt, more important perhaps to Muslim sentiment?

The anthropomorphic form encouraged stories of the nose being knocked off and the piercing of the belly from which jewels poured forth.[18] Fantasizing on the wealth of the temples evoked a vision of immense opulence, and this could suggest that the Turkish invasions were a veritable 'gold-rush'.[19] One account states that the image contained twenty *man* of jewels — one *man* weighing several kilograms; another, that a gold chain weighing two hundred *man* kept the image in place. Yet another describes the icon as made of iron with a magnet placed above it, so that it would be suspended in space, an awesome sight for the worshipper.[20] The age of the temple is taken further and further back in time until it is described as thirty thousand years old. One wonders if Somanātha was not becoming something of a fantasy in such accounts.

More purposive writing of the fourteenth century are the chronicles of Baranī and Iṣāmī. Both were poets, one associated with the Delhi Sultanate and the other with the Bahmani kingdom of the Deccan. Both project Maḥmūd as the ideal Muslim hero, but somewhat differently. Baranī states that his writing is intended to educate Muslim rulers in their duties towards Islam.[21] For him, religion and kingship are twins and the ruler needs to

---

Presidency, I, 523; Eliot and Dowson, II, 248 ff; 468 ff. Al Kazwini, Eliot and Dowson, I 97 ff. Abdullah Wassaf, Eliot and Dowson, III, 44 ff; IV. 181.

[18] Attar quoted in Nazim, op. cit., 221; Firishta in J. Briggs, *History of the Rise of the Mohammadan Power in India*, Calcutta, 1966 (reprint).

[19] A. Wink, *Al-Hind*, volume II, 124 ff.

[20] Zakariya al Kazvini, *Asarul-bilad*, Eliot and Dowson, op. cit., I, 97 ff.

[21] *Fatāwa-yi-Jahāndārī* discussed in P. Hardy, *Historians of Medieval India*, Delhi, 1997 (repr.), 25 ff; 107 ff.

know the religious ideals of kingship if he claims to be ruling on behalf of God. Sultans must protect Islam through the *sharī'a* and destroy both Muslim heretics and infidels. Maḥmūd is said to be the ideal ruler because he did both.

Iṣāmī composes what he regards as an epic poem on the Muslim rulers of India, on the lines of the famous Persian poet Firdausī's earlier epic on the Persian kings, the *Shāh-nāma*. Iṣāmī argues that kingship descended from God, first to the pre-Islamic rulers of Persia — in which he includes Alexander of Macedon and the Sassanid kings, and subsequently to the Sultans of India, with Maḥmūd establishing Muslim rule in India.[22] Interestingly the Arabs, who had both a political and economic presence in the sub-continent prior to Maḥmūd, hardly figure in this history. That there is a difference of perception in these narratives, is important to a historical assessment and requires further investigation.

The role of Maḥmūd it would seem, was also undergoing a change from being viewed merely as an iconoclast to also being projected as the founder of an Islamic state in India, even if the latter statement was not historically accurate. Presumably given his status in Islamic historiography this was a form of indirectly legitimizing the Sultans in India. The appropriation of the pre-Islamic Persian rulers for purposes of legitimacy, suggests that there may have been an element of doubt about the accepted role-models of Muslim rulers. The Sultans in India were not only ruling a society substantially of non-Muslims, but even those who had converted to Islam were in large part following the customary practices of their *zāt*, their erstwhile caste, which were often not in conformity with the *sharī'a*. Is there then a hint of an underlying uncertainty, of a lack of confidence, in the insistence on taking

[22] *Futūḥ-al-Salāṭīn* discussed in Hardy, op. cit., 107–8.

Islamic rule back to Maḥmūd, a champion of the Islamic world? Can we say that these accounts had converted the event itself at Somanātha, into what some today would call, an icon?

In the post-fourteenth century, narratives of the event continue with still greater embellishments and these are perhaps what we would see as a cloud of hype. Of the actual temple the impression sought to be created is that it never recovered from the raid and ceased to be important. Yet every few decades some Sultan is said to have attacked the Somanātha temple and converted it into a mosque.[23] Logically therefore, and logic is not at a premium in these accounts, they would, after the first attack, be attacking a mosque. In a sense the claim ceases to be history and becomes rhetoric. Nor does this stop Sanskrit texts from continuing to refer to it as a temple, a holy city, a second Kailāśa.[24] Was this a parallel situation to the mosque-church toggle-switching at places such as Cordoba in Spain and Santa Sophia in Istanbul, each time the area changed rulers or a religion receded?

Let me turn now to the Jaina texts of this period. These, not unexpectedly associate a different set of concerns with the event, or else they ignore it. The eleventh century Jaina poet from the Paramāra court in Malwa, Dhanapāla, a contemporary of Maḥmūd, briefly mentions Maḥmūd's campaign in Gujarat and his raids on various places including Somanātha.[25] He comments however, at much greater length on Maḥmūd's inability to damage the icons of Mahāvīra in Jaina temples for, as he puts it, snakes

[23] Dhaky and Sastri, op. cit.

[24] Ibid.

[25] *Satyapurīya-Mahāvīra-utsaha*, III.2. D. Sharma, 'Some New Light on the Route of Mahmud of Ghazni's Raid on Somanātha: Multan to Somanātha and Somanātha to Multan', in B.P. Sinha (ed.), *Dr Satkari Mookerji Felicitation Volume*, Varanasi, 1969, 165–8.

cannot swallow Garuḍa nor can stars dim the light of the sun. This for him is proof of the superior power of the Jaina images as compared to the Śaiva, the latter having been descecrated.

In the early twelfth century, another Jaina text informs us that the Caulukya king, angered by the *rākṣasas*, the *daityas* and the *asuras* who were destroying temples and disturbing the *ṛṣis* and *brāhmaṇas*, campaigned against them.[26] One expects the list to include the Turuṣkas as the Turks were called, but instead mention is made of the local *rājās*. The king is said to have made a pilgrimage to Somanātha and found that the temple was old and was disintegrating. He is said to have stated that it was a disgrace that the local *rājās* were plundering the pilgrims to Somanātha but could not keep the temple in good repair. This is the same king who built a mosque at Cambay, which mosque was later destroyed in a campaign against the Caulukyas of Gujarat by the Paramāras of Malwa. But the Paramāra king also looted the Jaina and other temples built under the patronage of the Caulukyas.[27] It would seem that when the temple was seen as a statement of power, it could become a target of attack, irrespective of religious affiliations.

In the late twelfth century during the reign of the famous Caulukya king, Kumārapāla, there is much activity around the Somanātha temple. Among the ministers of Kumārapāla was Hemacandra; a respected and erudite scholar of Jaina religious history, and incidentally a rival of the Śaiva Pāśupata chief priest of the Somanātha temple, Bhāva Bṛhaspati. Such Śaiva–Jaina rivalry was known to other parts of the sub-continent as well. There is

[26] Hemacandra, *Dvyāśrāya-kāvya*, in *Indian Antiquary* 1875, 4, 72 ff, 110 ff, 232 ff, 265 ff; Ibid.; J. Klatt, 'Extracts from the Historical Records of the Jainas', *Indian Antiquary* 1882, 11, 245–56.

[27] P. Bhatia, *The Paramaras*, Delhi, 1970, 141.

therefore some discrepancy between the statements of the minister and the chief priest.

Various Jaina texts, giving the history of Kumārapāla mention his connection with Somanātha. It is stated that he wished to be immortalized.[28] So Hemacandra persuaded the king to replace the dilapidated temple at Somanātha with a new stone temple. The temple is clearly described as dilapidated and not destroyed. When the new temple on the location of the old had been completed, both Kumārapāla and Hemacandra took part in the ritual of consecration. Hemacandra wished to impress the king with the spiritual powers of a Jaina *ācārya*, so on his bidding Śiva, the deity of the temple, appeared before the king. Kumārapāla was so overcome by this miracle that he converted to the Jaina faith. The focus again is on the superior power of Jainism over Śaivism. The renovating of the temple which is also important, takes on the symbolism of political legitimation for the king. It does seem curious that these activities focused on the Somanātha temple, yet no mention is made of Maḥmūd, in spite of the raid having occurred in the previous couple of centuries. The miracle is the central point in the connection with Somanātha in these accounts.

Some suggestion of an anguish over what may be indirect references to the raids of Maḥmūd come from quite other Jaina sources and interestingly these relate to the merchant community. In an anthology of stories, one refers to the merchant Jāvaḍi, who quickly makes a fortune in trade and then goes in search of a Jaina icon which had been taken away to the land called Gajjana.[29] This is clearly Ghazna. The ruler of Gajjana was a Yavana — a term by

[28] Merutunga, *Prabandha-cintāmaṇi*, C.H. Tawney (trans), Calcutta, 1899, IV, 129 ff. G. Buhler, *The Life of Hemacandracarya*, Shantiniketan, 1936.

[29] *Nābhinandanoddhāra*, discussed in P. Granoff, 'The Householder as Shaman: Jaina Biographies of Temple Builders', *East and West*, 42, 1992, 2–4, 301–17.

now used for those coming from the west. The Yavana ruler was easily won over by the wealth presented to him by Jāvaḍi. He allowed Jāvaḍi to search for the icon and when it was found, gave him permission to take it back. Not only that but the Yavana worshipped the icon prior to its departure. The second part of the narrative deals with the vicissitudes of having the icon installed in Gujarat, but that is another story.

This is a reconciliation story with a certain element of wishful thinking. The initial removal of the icon is hurtful and creates anguish. Its return should ideally be through reconciling iconoclasts to the worship of icons. There are other touching stories in which the ruler of Gajjana or other Yavana kings are persuaded not to attack Gujarat. But such stories are generally related as a demonstration of the power of the Jaina *ācāryas*.

The Jaina sources therefore underline their own ideology. Jaina temples survive, Śaiva temples get destroyed. Śiva has abandoned his icons unlike Mahāvīra who still resides in his icons and protects them. Attacks are to be expected in the Kaliyuga — the present age — since it is an age of evil. Icons will be broken but wealthy Jaina merchants will restore the temple and the icons will invariably and miraculously, mend themselves.

The argument about Kaliyuga and iconoclasm also occurs in the *Purāṇas*, where an increasing decline in *dharma* accompanies the passing of the cycle of time. Deities desert their icons in the Kaliyuga especially if kings are not attentive enough to them.[30] Sometimes there is a mention of temples being destroyed but generally they are said to have been dilapidated and neglected —

[30] P. Granoff, 'Tales of Broken Limbs and Bleeding Wounds: Responses to Muslim Iconoclasm in Medieval India', *East and West*, 41, 1991, 1–4, 182–203. *Vāyu Purāṇa*, I. 58. 31–74; II. 36. 115–25.

as would be expected in an age of declining virtue — and therefore requiring repair. The association with Kaliyuga gives the situation a feeling of infallibility. Kaliyuga is therefore a partial but generalized reference to the vulnerability of the practice and symbol of *dharma*. What remains curious is the lack of specific mention about Maḥmūd's raid on Somanātha, which in the Turko-Persian chronicles is so central.

The third category of major narratives is constituted by the inscriptions in Sanskrit from Somanātha itself, focusing on the temple and its vicinity. The perspectives which these point to are again very different from the earlier two. In the twelfth century the Caulukya king, Kumārapāla, issues an inscription. He appoints a governor to protect Somanātha and the protection is against the piracy and the looting by the local *rājās*.[31] A century later, the Caulukyas are again protecting the site, this time from attacks by the Malwa *rājās*.[32] The regular complaint about local *rājās* looting pilgrims at Somanātha becomes a continuing refrain in many inscriptions.

In 1169, an inscription records the appointment of the chief priest of the Somanātha temple, Bhāva Bṛhaspati.[33] He claims to have come from Kannauj, from a family of Pāśupata Śaiva *brāhmaṇas* and, as the inscriptions show, initiated a succession of powerful priests at the Somanātha temple. He states that he was sent by Śiva himself to rehabilitate the temple. This was required because it was an old structure, much neglected by the officers and because temples in any case deteriorate in the Kaliyuga. Bhāva

[31] Praci Inscription, *Poona Orienalist*, 1937, 1.4. 39–46.
[32] *Epigraphia Indica*, II, 437 ff.
[33] Prabhaspattana Inscription, *BPSI*, 186.

Bṛhaspati claims that it was he who persuaded Kumārapāla to replace the older wooden temple with a stone temple.

Again no mention is made of the raid of Maḥmūd. Was this out of embarrassment, that a powerful icon of Śiva had been desecrated? Or was the looting of a temple not such an extraordinary event? The Turko-Persian chronicles may well have been indulging in exaggeration. Yet the looting of the pilgrims by the local *rājās* is repeatedly mentioned. Was Kumārapāla's renovation both an act of veneration of Śiva but also a seeking of legitimation? Was this in a sense an inversion of Maḥmūd seeking legitimation through raiding the temple? Are these then counter-points of legitimation in viewing the past?

In 1264, a long legal document was issued in the form of an inscription with both a Sanskrit and an Arabic version and concerns the acquisition of land and the building of a mosque by a trader from Hormuz.[34] Being a legal document it was dated in four current dating systems — Hijrī, Saṁvat, Siṁha and Valabhī. The Sanskrit version begins with the usual formulaic symbol — the *siddham* — and continues with invoking Viśvanātha, a name for Śiva. But there is also a suggestion that it was a rendering into Sanskrit of Allah, the Lord of the Universe. The parallelism is striking at more than one place in the inscription and can be viewed as yet another example of cultural translation. We are told that Khoja Noradina Piroja/Nuruddin Feruz, the son of Khoja Nau Abu Brahima of Hurmujadeśa/Hormuz, a *nakhuda* or commander of a ship, a *sadr*/chief and evidently a respected trader — as his title Khoja/Khwajah, would indicate — acquired land in Mahājanapālī on the outskirts of the town of Somanātha, to build a mosque, which is referred to as a *mijigiti*/*masjid*, and described as a *dharmasthāna*. The land was acquired from the local *rājā*, Srī

[34]Somanathapattana Veraval Inscription, *Epigraphia Indica*, XXXIV, 141 ff.

Chāḍā, son of Nānasiṁha, and reference is also made to the governor of Kathiawar, the *mahāmātya* Māladeva, and the Caulukya–Vaghela king, Arjunadeva.

The acquisition of this land has the approval of two local bodies — the *pañcakula* and the association of the *jamātha*. The *pañcakulas* were powerful administrative and local committees, well-established by this period, consisting of recognized authorities such as priests, officers, merchants, local dignitaries. This particular *pañcakula* was headed by the Para/*purohita* Vīrabadhra, the Śaiva Pāśupata *ācārya* most likely of the Somanātha temple, and among its members was the merchant Abhyasiṁha. From other inscriptions it would seem that Para Vīrabhadra was related to Bhāva Bṛhaspati in a line of succession. The witnesses to this agreement of granting land for the building of the mosque are mentioned by name and described as the *bṛhat-puruṣa*, literally 'the big men'. They were the *Ṭhakkuras*, *Rāṇakas*, *Rājās* and merchants, many from the Mahājanapālī. Some of these dignitaries were functionaries of the estates of the Somanātha and other temples. The land given for the mosque in Mahājanapālī was part of these estates.

The other committee endorsing the agreement was the *jamātha*, consisting of ship-owners, artisans, sailors and religious teachers, probably from Hormuz. Also mentioned are the oil-millers, masons and Musalmāna horse-handlers, all referred to by what appear to be occupational or caste names, such as *cūnākāra* and *ghamcika*. Were these local converts to Islam? Since the *jamātha* was to ensure these endowments for the maintenance of the mosque, it was necessary to indicate its membership.

The inscription lists the endowments for the mosque. These included two large measures of land which were part of the temple property from adjoining temples situated in Somanātha-pattana; land from a *maṭha*; income from two shops in the vicinity; and an oil mill. The measures of land were bought from the *purohita* and the chief priests of the temples and the sales were attested by the men of rank. The shops and the oil-mill were purchased from the local people. One of the chief priests, Tripurāntaka, seems to appear again, twenty-three years later, in a number of inscriptions as a wealthy and powerful Pāśupata Śaiva priest who built many temples in the vicinity.[35] As with many Sanskirt votive inscriptions, it ends with the hope that the terms and conditions of the agreement may last as long as the moon and sun endure

The tone and sentiment of the inscription is amicable and clearly the settlement had been agreed to on all sides. The building of a substantial mosque in association with some of the properties of the Somanātha temple, not by a conqueror but by a trader through a legal agreement, was obviously not objected to, neither by the local governor and dignitaries nor by the priests, all of whom were party to the decision. The mosque is thus closely linked to the erstwhile properties and the functionaries of the Somanātha temple.

This raises many questions. Did this transaction, two hundred or so years after the raid of Maḥmūd, not interfere with the remembrance of the raid as handed down, in the minds of the priests and the local 'big men'? Were memories short or was the event relatively unimportant?

Nuruddin Feroz used Sanskrit and Arabic for the agreement, Sanskrit as the local formal language and Arabic probably as the language of incoming traders. The two texts are by and large similar but not identical. The Arabic version carries the hope that the people of Somanātha will convert to Islam — a statement which is wisely deleted in the Sanskrit version. The use of Arabic points to a specific identity distinct from the use of Persian in

[35] The Cintra *Praśasti*, *Epigraphia Indica*, I, 271 ff.

connection with Maḥmūd. Did the local people make a distinction between the Arab and west Asian traders on the one hand — often referred to as Tājikas, and Turks or Turuṣkas on the other? And were the former acceptable and the Turks much less so? Clearly they were not all homogenized and identified as 'Muslims', as we would do today. Should we not sift the reactions to the event by examining the responses of particular social groups and situations? Hormuz was crucial to the horse trade, therefore Nuruddin was welcomed. Did the profits of trade over-rule other considerations? Were the temples and their administrators also investing in horse trading and making handsome profits?

In the fifteenth century a number of short inscriptions from Gujarat refer the battles against the Turks. One very moving inscription in Sanskrit comes from Somanātha itself.[36] Although written in Sanskrit, it begins with the Islamic formulaic blessing — *bismillah rahman-i-rahim*. It gives details of the family of the Vohara/Bohra Farīd and the Bohras were of Arab descent. We are told that the town of Somanātha was attacked by the Turuṣkas, the Turks, and Vohara Farīd who was the son of Vohara Muhammad, joined in the defence of the town, fighting against the Turuṣkas on behalf of the local ruler Brahmadeva. Farīd was killed and the inscription is a memorial to him.

It would seem from the sources that I have tried to place before you, that the aftermath of the raid of Maḥmūd on the temple of Somanātha took the form of varying perceptions of the event, and different from what we have assumed. There are no simplistic explanations that would emerge from any or all of these narratives. How then have we arrived today at the rather simplistic historical

[36] D.B. Disalkar, 'Inscriptions of Kathiawad', *New Indian Antiquary*, 1939, 1, 591.

theory that the raid of Maḥmūd created a trauma in the Hindu consciousness which has been at the root of Hindu–Muslim relations ever since. Or to put it in the words of K.M. Munshi, 'For a thousand years Maḥmūd's destruction of the shrine has been burnt into the collective subconscious of the [Hindu] race as an unforgettable national disaster'.[37]

Interestingly, what appears to be the earliest mention of a 'Hindu trauma' in connection with Maḥmūd's raid on Somanātha, comes from the debate in the House of Commons in London in 1843, on the question of the gates of the Somanātha temple.[38] In 1842, Lord Ellenborough issued his famous 'Proclamation of the Gates' in which he ordered General Nott, in charge of the British Army in Afghanistan, to return via Ghazni and bring back to India the sandalwood gates from the tomb of Maḥmūd. There were believed to have been looted by Maḥmūd from Somanātha. It was claimed that the intention was to return what was looted from India, an act which would symbolize British control over Afghanistan despite their poor showing in the Anglo–Afghan wars. It was also presented as an attempt to reverse Indian subjugation to Afghanistan in the pre-British period. Was this an appeal to Hindu sentiment, as some maintained?

The Proclamation raised a storm in the House of Commons and became a major issue in the cross-fire between the Government and the Opposition. The question was asked whether Ellenborough was catering to religious prejudices by appeasing the Hindus or was he appealing to national sympathies. It was

[37] Munshi, op. cit., 89.

[38] *The United Kingdom House of Commons Debate, March 9, 1943,* on, The Somnath [Prabhās Patan] Proclamation, Junagadh 1948, 584–602, 620, 630–2, 656, 674.

defended by those who maintained that the gates were a 'national trophy' and not a religious icon. In this connection the request of Ranjit Singh, the ruler of the Punjab, to the king of Afghanistan, Shah Shujah, for the return of the gates, was quoted. But on examining the letter making this request, it was discovered that Ranjit Singh had confused the Somanātha temple with the Jagannātha temple. It was also argued that no historian mentions the gates in the various accounts of Maḥmūd's raid, therefore the story of the gates could only be an invention of folk tradition.

The historians referred to were Gibbon who wrote on the Roman empire, Firdausī and Sa'dī — both Persian poets, and Firishta. The last of these was the only one who, in the seventeenth century had written on Indian history. Firishta was well-known because Alexander Dow had translated his history into English in the late eighteenth century. Firishta's account of the sack of Somanātha was as fanciful as the earlier accounts, with obvious exaggerations such as the huge size of the idol and the quantity of jewels that poured out when Maḥmūd pierced its belly. Members of the House of Commons were using their perceptions of Indian history as ammunition in their own political and party hostilities.

Those critical of Ellenborough were fearful of the consequences; they saw the fetching of the gates as supporting a native religion, and that too, the monstrous 'Liṅga-ism' as they called it; and they felt that its political consequences would be violent indignation among the Mohammadans. Those supporting Ellenborough, in the House of Commons, argued equally vehemently, that he was removing the feeling of degradation from the minds of the Hindus. It would, '. . . relieve that country, which had been overrun by the Mohammadan conqueror, from the painful feelings which had been rankling amongst the people for nearly a thousand years'. And that, '. . . the memory of the gates [has been] preserved by the Hindus as a painful memorial of the most devastating invasions that had ever desolated Hindustan.'

Ellenborough saw Maḥmūd's raid on Somanātha as embedded in the Hindu psyche and the return of the gates he felt would avenge the insult of eight hundred years.[39] Did this debate fan an anti-Muslim Hindu sentiment among Hindus in India, which, judging from the earlier sources, had either not existed, or been marginal and localized? The absence in earlier times of an articulation of a trauma, remains enigmatic.

The gates were uprooted and brought back in triumph. But on arrival they were found to be of Egyptian workmanship and not associated in any way with India. So they were placed in a storeroom in the Agra Fort and possibly by now have been eaten by white ants.

From this point on, the arguments of the debate in the House of Commons come to be reflected in the writing on Somanātha. Maḥmūd's raid was made into the central point in Hindu–Muslim relations. K.M. Munshi led the demand for the restoration of the Somanātha temple. His obsession with restoring the glories of Hindu history, began in a general way with his writing historical novels, inspired by reading Walter Scot. But the deeper imprint came from his familiarity with Bankim Chandra Chatterji's sentiments in *Ānandamaṭha*,[40] as is evident from his novel, *Jaya Somanātha*, published in 1927. And as one historian, R.C. Majumdar puts it, Bankim Chandra's nationalism was Hindu rather than Indian. 'This is made crystal clear from his other writings which contain passionate outbursts against the subjugation of India by

[39] R.H. Davis, op. cit., 202.
[40] Pers. com. U. Joshi

the Muslims'.[41] Bankim Chandra was not alone in being hostile to both British and Muslim rule. Munshi was concerned with restoring the Hindu Aryan glory of the pre-Islamic past. Muslim rule was viewed as the major disjuncture in Indian history. Munshi's comments often echo the statements made in the House of Commons debate as is evident from his book, *Somanatha — The Shrine Eternal.*

His insistence that the temple be restored led to the excavation of the site in 1950, the results of which contradicted much of what he maintained. The reconstruction through archaeology and architectural history indicated an original temple of the ninth or tenth century, more likely the latter, with some signs of desecration.[42] An eleventh century temple was rebuilt on the earlier plan and this structure was replaced in about the twelfth century. There is little evidence of later structures of importance or major reconstructions.

Munshi made the Somanātha temple into the most important symbol of Muslim iconoclasm in India. But prior to this, its significance appears to have been largely regional. Consistent references to it as a symbol of Muslim iconoclasm are to be found largely only in the Turko-Persian chronicles. Possibly the fact that Munshi was himself from Gujarat may have had some role in his projection of Somanātha. In other parts of the country the symbols of iconoclasm, where they existed, were places of local importance and knowledge of the raid on Somanātha was of marginal interest.

On the rebuilding of the Somanātha temple in 1951, Munshi, by then a minister of the central government had this to say: '. . . the collective subconscious of India today is happier with the

[41] R.C. Majumdar, *British Paramountcy and Indian Renaissance*, Part II, History and Culture of the Indian People, 1965, Bombay, 478.

[42] B.K. Thapar, op. cit.

scheme of the reconstruction of Somanātha, sponsored by the Government of India, than with many other things we have done or are doing.'[43] Nehru objected strongly to the Government of India being associated with the project and insisted on its being restored as a private venture.[44] That the President of India, Rajendra Prasad was to perform the consecration ceremony was even more unacceptable to him. He was further irritated by Munshi writing to Indian ambassadors in various parts of the world, asking for jars of water from the rivers of the countries to which they were accredited as also a variety of plants, to be sent to India — presumably via the diplomatic bag — and all of which were said to be necessary to the consecration ceremony of the reconstructed temple. The ceremony itself was attended by a few stalwart nationalists some associated with the government, thus providing a hint of some of their substratum concerns. This introduces a further dimension to the reading of the event, involving the secular credentials of society and state.

The received opinion is that events such as the raid on Somanātha created what has been called, two antagonistic categories of epic: the 'epic of conquest' and the 'counter-epic of resistance'.[45] It has also been thought of as epitomizing in later Turko-Persian narratives 'the archetypal encounter of Islam with Hindu idolatry'.[46] We may well ask how and when did this dichotomy crystallize? Did it emerge with modern historians reading too literally from just one set of narratives, without juxtaposing these with the other

[43] Munshi, op. cit., 184.

[44] S. Gopal (ed.), *Selected Works of Jawaharlal Nehru*, vol. 16, Part I, Delhi, 1994, 270 ff.

[45] Aziz Ahmed, 'Epic and Counter-Epic in Medieval India', *Journal of the American Oriental Society*, 83, 1963, 470–6.

[46] Davis, op. cit., 93.

narratives? If narratives are read without being placed in a historiographical context, the reading is, to put it mildly, incomplete and therefore distorted. Firishta's version for example, was repeated endlessly in recent times, without considering its historiography: neither was this done within the tradition of the Turko-Persian chronicles nor in the context of other narratives which can be said to impinge on the same event. Or, has the dichotomy becomes such a mind set that we are unable to comprehend the complexities and nuances of the representations of an event, and its aftermath, however familiar they may be?

We continue to see such situations as a binary projection of Hindu and Muslim. Yet what should be evident from the sources which I have discussed is that there are multiple groups with varying agendas, involved in the way in which the event and Somanātha are represented. There are differentiations in the attitudes of the Persian chronicles towards the Arabs and the Turks. Within the Persian sources, the earlier fantasy of Manāt gradually gives way to a more political concern with the legitimacy of Islamic rule in India through the Sultans. Was there, on the part of the Persian chroniclers, a deliberate down-playing of the Arab intervention in India? Were the politics of heresy and revolt in the history of Islam at this period, linked to these attitudes? The hostility between the Bohras and the Turks, technically both Muslims, may have also been part of this confrontation since the Bohras had some Arab ancestry and probably saw themselves as among the settled communities of Gujarat and saw the Turks as invaders.

Biographies and histories from Jaina authors, discussing matters pertaining to the royal court and to the religion of the elite, focus on attempts to show Mahāvīra in a better light than Śiva and the agenda becomes that of the competing rivalry between the Jainas and the Śaivas. But the sources which focus on a different social group, that of the Jaina merchants, seem to be conciliatory towards the confrontation with Maḥmūd, perhaps because the trading community would have suffered heavy disruptions in periods of raids and campaigns.

From the Veraval inscription of 1264, co-operation in the building of the mosque came from a range of social groups, from the most orthodox ritual specialists to those wielding secular authority and from the highest property holders to those with lesser property. Interestingly, the local members of the *jamātha*, if they were all Muslims — as is likely — were largely from occupations at the lower end of the social scale. As such, their responsibility for the maintenance of the mosque would have required the goodwill of the Somanātha elite. Did the elite see themselves as patrons of a new kind of control over property?

These relationships were not determined by the general category of what have been called Hindu interests and Muslim interests. They varied in accordance with more particular interests and these drew on identities of ethnicity, economic concerns, religious sectarianism and social status.

Let me conclude by briefly returning to my initial comments on narrative and history. There are those who argue that narrative speaks for itself and does not require historians to interpret it. But narrative does not speak, it is spoken. The historian in giving a voice to the narrative invests it with nuances, emphases and interpretations. This is inevitably a different voice from that of the poet, the dramatist, the chronicler, although there may be points of fusion. The recognition of differences, it seems to me enriches the reading. We need to understand why there are variants and what is their individual agenda. Even in fictionalized accounts there is a politics in the telling and the retelling, as I have tried to show in the first lecture. This becomes more evident where diverse narratives are wrapped around what might relate to the same event.

Different narratives reconstitute events in different ways. Narratives involve an interface with the historical moment and encapsulate ideological structures. All narrative representations do not have an equal validity even if a single, authentic, foundational narrative cannot be identified. Merely to analyse fragments cannot be the end purpose of writing history. The priorities used by the historian in explaining the narratives becomes relevant and can suggest the inter-links and patterns emerging from the fragments. The narrative can also stretch its presuppositions over a long duration of time and move across this duration; as indeed each narrative can present a different image.

In the retelling of an event, there may be a claim that it encapsulates memory or a succession of memories: so too the question of whether or why there may be an amnesia. Memory is sometimes claimed in order to create an identity, and history based on such claims is used to legitimize the identity. Establishing a fuller understanding of the event is crucial in both instances, for otherwise the identity and its legitimation, can be historically invalid.

I have tried to show how each set of narratives turn the focus of what Somanātha symbolizes: the occasion for the projection of an iconoclast and champion of Islam; the assertion of the superiority of Jainism over Śaivism; the inequities of the Kaliyuga; the centrality of the profits of trade subordinating other considerations; colonial perceptions of Indian society as having always been an antagonistic duality of Hindu and Muslim; Hindu nationalism and the restoration of a particular view of the past contesting the secularizing of modern Indian society. But these are not discrete foci. Even when juxtaposed, a pattern emerges; a pattern which requires that the understanding of the event should be historically contextual, multi-faceted, and aware of the ideological structures implicit in the narratives.

I would argue that Mahmūd of Ghazni's raid on the Somanātha temple, did not create a dichotomy, because each of the many facets involved in the perception of the event, consciously or sub-consciously, was enveloped in a multiplicity of other contexts as well. These direct our attention to varying representations, both overt and hidden, and lead us to explore the statements implicit in these representations. The assessment of these facets may provide us with more sensitive insights into our past.

Index

Abhinavagupta 14
Ābhīras 27
Afghanistan 42
agrahāras 9, 11
ākhyāna 5
Alberuni 27
Ānanadavardhana 14
Arab 26, 47
Arabic 40
araṇya 11
āśrama 9ff, 11, 12ff
āṭavikas 12

Bankim Chandra Chatterji 44ff
bārahmāsā 14
Baranī 31
Bharata 6ff, 10
Bhāva Bṛhaspati 37ff
brāhmaṇas 29
Braj-*bhāṣā* 14

Caliphate 29
Cambay 26, 34
Caulukyas 25, 27, 34, 37
Chāvḍa 27
China 27
clans 9
colonial 22
court 13
Cūḍasamas 27
culture 5

dāstān 15
Dehlavi 15
Dhanapāla 33
Dow, A. 43
Duḥṣanta/ Duṣyanta 6, 10ff, 19ff
Durlabha 27
Durvāsas 10

Ellenborough, Lord 42ff
excavation of Somanātha 45

Farrukh Siyar 14
Farrukhī Sīstānī 28
Firishta 43, 47
Firdausī 43

gāndharva 6, 8, 12, 18
gates of Somanātha 42, 44
gender 4, 22
Ghazni 26
Gibbon 43
Goethe 16, 21
grāma 11
Gujarat 30

Hastināpura 6, 11
Hemacandra 35
Hindu/s 19, 42

Hobsbawm, E. 2
Hormuz 26, 38
horse/s 26, 30, 41
House of Commons 42–3

iconoclasm 45
Indian Shakespeare, The 16
Indra 10
Iṣāmī 31ff
Islam 40
Ismā'īlīs 29–30

Jaina 27, 33, 35ff, 47ff
jamātha 39, 48
Jāvaḍi 36
Jaya Somanātha 44
Jones, Sir William 15
Judeo-Christian 17, 20

Kālidāsa 8ff, 23
Kaliyuga 36–7
Kaṇva 6, 11–12
Kathā 14
Kathāsarītasagāra 13
Kaṭṭahāri Jātaka 9
Khoja Noradina Piroja 38, 41
kṣetra 11
Kumārapāla 34–5, 37ff

land 9
lingam 27ff, 30
literature 3

Mahābhārata 5ff, 22ff, 25
Mahājanapālī 39
Mahāvīra 47
Maḥmūd 24ff, 27ff, 31
Majumdar R.C. 44
Manāt 28ff, 31
Manṣūra 30
Mārīca 10
memory 49
Menakā 6
middle class 20
Mill, James 18
Mohammad 28
Monier-Williams, M. 18ff
morality 19, 21
mosque 34, 38, 48
Multan 27ff, 30
Munshi, K.M. 42, 44ff

nāṭaka 14
nationalism 20ff
nature 12, 16
Nāṭyaśāstra 14
Neo-Platonists 17

oil-mill 40
Orientalism 18, 21
Orientalist 5, 19
Oriental Renaissance 16

pañcakula 39
Paramāras 34
pativratā 7, 12
patriarchy 13
Persian chronicles 47
piracy 27
Prabhās 25
Purāṇas 8, 13

Qur'ān 28

race science 17
Rāghavabhaṭṭa 14

Rajendra Prasad 64
Ranjit Singh 43
rasa 14
ring 10
Romanticism 16ff, 22

Sa'dī 28, 43
Śaiva 25, 37
Śaiva Pāśupata 34, 37ff
saṃbhoga śṛṅgāra 12
Sanskrit 40–1
Saurashtra 25
Schubert, F. 16
sharī'a
Shias 30
shops 39
Sind 30
Śiva 31, 36–8, 47
Stone, L. 2
Sultan 33
Sunni 29

Tagore, R. 20
Tairoff 16
Tājika 26, 41
tapasya 21
taxes 26
trade 25–6
Tripurāntaka 40
Turko-Persian 47
Turks 34, 47
Turuṣkas 41

Urdu 15

vana 11
Veraval 26ff
vipralamba śṛṅgāra 12
Vīrabadhra 39
Viśvāmitra 6
Vohara\Bohra 41, 47

wealth 31
women/woman 20ff

Yādavas 27
Yavana 35

Zanzibar 27
zāt 32